Dedicated to the resonantly brave.

M.D. Tophus

Gaslighting.

Copyright ©. 2023. M.D. Tophus. All rights reserved

Hilphma Publications 2023. www.hilphmapublication.com

First Edition.

Germany.

The author has over 25 years of clinical experience in the healthcare field. Is cognisant of both DSM-5-TR (and previous versions) and ICD-11 (and previous versions) disorders and conditions; quality and safety improvement in healthcare; and healthcare education

Other M.D. Tophus publications available:

"Exercising Quality in Healthcare Service Provision: A Complex Care Workbook for All Healthcare Professionals." Germany: Hilphma Publications: 2022.

"Who is This Colleague?: Dangers of the Healthcare Profession, and beyond. An Interview Guide for Recruitment, Performance Appraisal and Post-Adverse Events."
Germany: Hilphma Publications: 2022.

"Think on your Feet: Those Who Can. For the Consummate Healthcare Professional."
Germany: Hilphma Publications: 2022.

"The Unfortunate Healthcare Treater, The Hapless Healthcare Therapist: Narcissistic and Borderline Personality Disorder clients. The Grit."
Germany: Hilphma Publications: 2022.

"Victims of Crime: Introduction to Forensic Challenges in Healthcare."
Germany: Hilphma Publications: 2022.

"The A to Z of Workplace Bullying: For the Healthcare Professional and Beyond."
Germany: Hilphma Publications: 2022.

"Trauma United, Life Defined. A Healthcare Tool for Professionals Across the Globe."
Germany: Hilphma Publications: 2022.

"Reflective Thinking: the True Healthcare Tool."
Germany: Hilphma Publications: 2022.

"Burnout in Healthcare."
Germany: Hilphma Publications: 2022.

"Reasonable Resilience in Workplaces and Healthcare Work."
Germany: Hilphma Publications: 2022.

"The Psychological Impacts of Labelling and Failure to Diagnose."
Germany: Hilphma Publications: 2022.

"The Controversy of the Remorseless and Unempathic Healthcare Worker."
Germany: Hilphma Publications: 2023.

"Attitudinal and Personality Traits in the Individual and Healthcare."
Germany: Hilphma Publications: 2023.

CONTENTS

Page

9   Introduction

11   Gaslighting Comprehensively Defined

15   Gaslighting in Personal Life (DV; Family; Friends)

22   Gaslighting in the Workplace; Patients; and Healthcare

25   Profiling Gaslighters

28   Gaslighting Indicators

31   Gaslighting Effects

34   Stages of Gaslighting. GHFSA: Grooming; Hostage to cruelty; Fragmentation; revelationary Shock; Aftermath

Stage 1: Grooming: 34

Stage 2: Hostage to cruelty: 36

Stage 3: Fragmentation: 37

Stage 4: revelationary Shock: 39

Stage 5: Aftermath: 41

43   **Identifying Gaslighting by Assessment**

46   **Gaslighting Case Scenarios: the Impacts:**

Case Scenario 1: 46

Case Scenario 2: 48

Case Scenario 3: 50

Case Scenario 4: 51

Questions- case scenarios: 52

53   **Key Points for Coping with Gaslighting**

56   **Abbreviations**

57   **Questions**

78   **References**

82   **Index**

Psychological manipulation, and abuse, takes many forms but in the context of gaslighting it strips the sufferer to the core- insidiously impacting the victim, often to the point of no return.

The secrecy, tactical manouevres, and seemingly pervasive style of abuse, perpetrated by the gaslighter creates gaslightee entrapment, perceptions of unreality and madness, with many sufferers being psychologically, emotionally, and physically, held in a hostage-like situation.

Much focus has been placed upon intimate partner based gaslighting. There exists however, a multitude of perpetrations involving friendship, familial, and institutional, gaslighting.

This publication includes concentration upon the personal, familial, parental, friendship, based gaslighting causes and impacts. So too, with regards to workplace settings, and healthcare environments. Profiling gaslighters, indicators, and effects, assessment measures, pertinent case scenarios, and coping strategies, are also of focus.
A newly created 5 victims' stages of the gaslighting process, is incorporated.
A comprehensive array of questions provides re-affirmation of the information provided.

Particularly relevant to this publication, as an additional and supportive resource, are the following:

"The A to Z of Workplace Bullying: For the Healthcare Professional and Beyond."
Germany: Hilphma Publications: 2022.

"Trauma United, Life Defined. A Healthcare Tool for Professionals Across the Globe." Germany: Hilphma Publications: 2022.

"The Psychological Impacts of Labelling and Failure to Diagnose".
Germany: Hilphma Publications: 2022.

"Burnout in Healthcare"
Germany: Hilphma Publications: 2022.

"The Controversy of the Remorseless and Unempathic Healthcare Worker"
Germany: Hilphma Publications: 2023.

GASLIGHTING COMPREHENSIVELY DEFINED

Gaslighting: was announced as the 'word of the year' in 2022 (1 a) the term is derived from the 1938 play (Gas Light); and the (1940 and) 1944 film called 'Gaslight'. (1 b)

Gaslighting is defined, as:

"to psychologically manipulate (a person) usually over an extended period of time so that the victim questions the validity of their own thoughts, perception of reality, or memories and experiences confusion, loss of confidence and self-esteem, uncertainty of one's emotional or mental stability, and a dependency on the perpetrator." (1 a)

To *Gaslight*, is:

"to manipulate another person into doubting his or her perceptions, experiences, or understanding of events. The term once referred to manipulation so extreme as to induce mental illness or to justify commitment of the gaslighted person to a psychiatric institution..." (2)

Gaslighting: Specific to workplace settings:

"Gaslighting: The ultimate aim is to make the victim question their sanity via psychological manipulation. It can involve the perpetrator denying that things took place (conversations, actions, and decisions); sabotage, or lying, so that one incurs the punishment for the gaslighter's errors; belittling of you in public; constant- daily- negative feedback about work performance; and creating a target of rumours and innuendo." (3)

Summarily, Gaslighting involves:

-the P of G (Perpetrator of Gaslighting) propagating trust in him/her as an authority figure

-which leads to the V of G (Victim of Gaslighting) constantly seeking approval

-direct or indirect manipulation and threats by P of G

-the V of G trusting in the gaslighter- more than one trusts oneself- and overtime self-trust dissipates to an all time low

-reliance on P of G's judgement about one's own mental state, capacity for memory, and beliefs about the relationship, other connections, and the world, ensues

-lack of contact with the outside world plus deteriorating self-esteem and increasing domination of the V of G, by the perpetrator, contributes to a cycle of gaslighting abuse which is affirmed as the norm.

It is argued that 'Stockholm syndrome' like symptoms play a part in many gaslighting relationships, whether personal or work related.

'Stockholm syndrome' like symptoms involve:

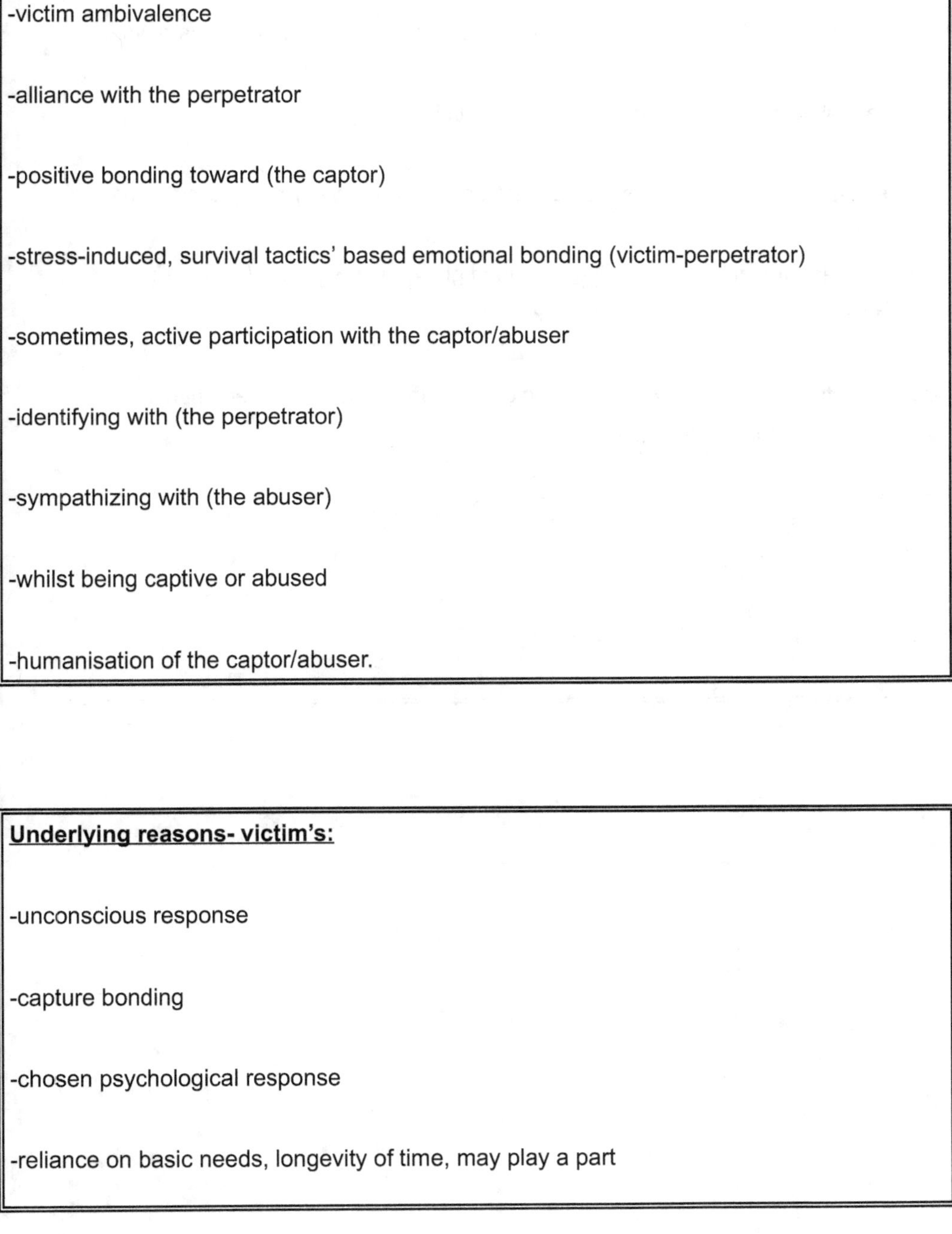

-victim ambivalence

-alliance with the perpetrator

-positive bonding toward (the captor)

-stress-induced, survival tactics' based emotional bonding (victim-perpetrator)

-sometimes, active participation with the captor/abuser

-identifying with (the perpetrator)

-sympathizing with (the abuser)

-whilst being captive or abused

-humanisation of the captor/abuser.

<u>**Underlying reasons- victim's:**</u>

-unconscious response

-capture bonding

-chosen psychological response

-reliance on basic needs, longevity of time, may play a part

-cognitive schema develops whereby 'us versus them' becomes the norm (captor/abuser and captive versus outside world/others/authority figures), traumatic reaction, depleted emotional resources, and increased vulnerability toward rapid brainwashing

-feelings of relief when not a subject of abusive actions, conceptualised as reward

-constant physical (or simulated physical) proximity

-de-escalatory appeasement of the abuser/captor becomes normalised over time

-cognitive-emotional bargaining (being a good girl, good boy), even conceptually, in desparation for release from the situation

-neuroplasticity, trauma based psychological preparedness, past attachments, and self-identity, factors (of the victim)

and,

-intermittent bad/good behaviors from captor.

Considered a form of psychological terrorism, gaslighting has significant impacts including effects on self-trust leading to doubt, ineffective decision making, and so many more deleterious impacts.

The P of Gs achieve this, by:

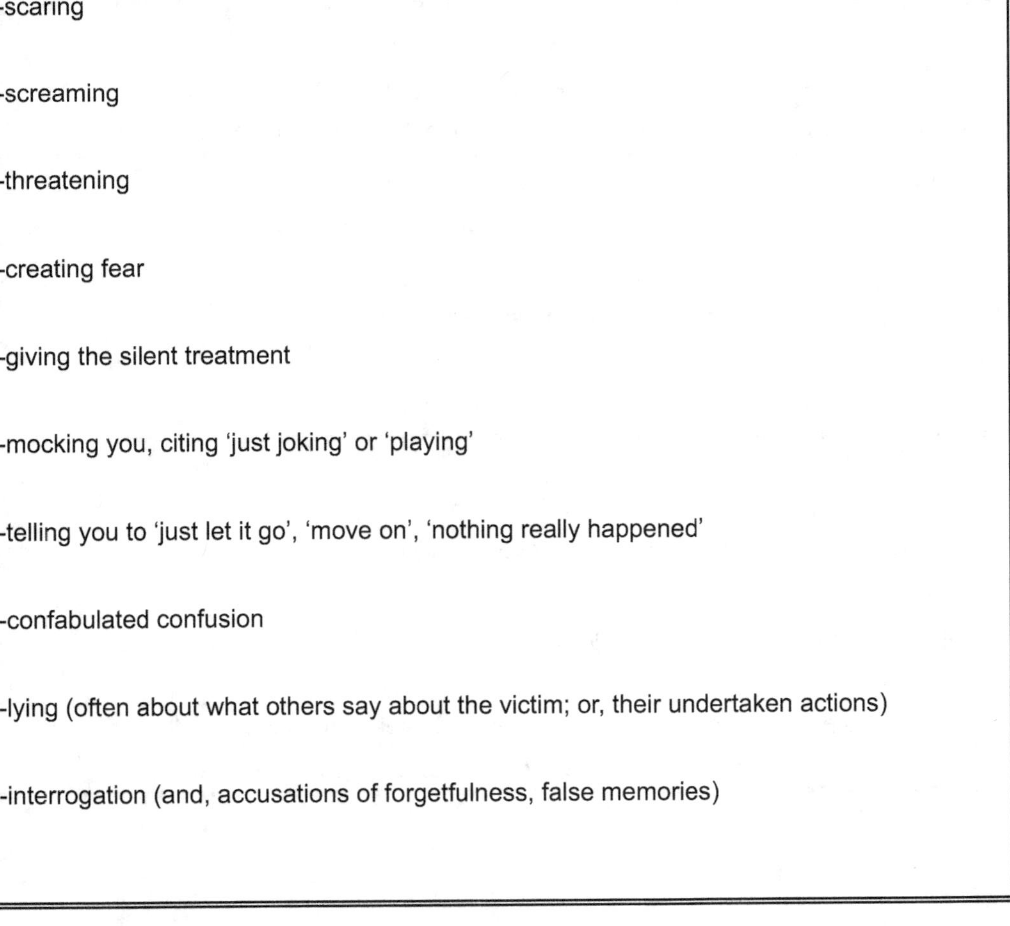

-scaring

-screaming

-threatening

-creating fear

-giving the silent treatment

-mocking you, citing 'just joking' or 'playing'

-telling you to 'just let it go', 'move on', 'nothing really happened'

-confabulated confusion

-lying (often about what others say about the victim; or, their undertaken actions)

-interrogation (and, accusations of forgetfulness, false memories)

-mimicking memory deficit (P of G denies that things proceeded as they did, or that the incident ever occurred)

-accusing the victim of having memory problems

-minimising and trivialising (accusations of V of G being over-sensitive, or stupid)

-expecting the victim to take responsibility for incidences (causing the victim to incessantly apologize)

-denial (the P of G refuses to take responsibility, uses projected blame)

-accusing the victim of lying, or borrowing someone else's story

-subtle to not so subtle, subversive threats that they (V of G) will not be believed if they seek outside help, use of gender, race, and so forth, to back up the argument.

Signs of gaslighting from (an abusive) partner:

In intimate relationships:

-stating that they are saying things out of love, and kindness

-being constantly told that you are imagining things

-loss of items believed to be misplaced and then reappear later on (one of the different types of attempts to make the victim believe that they are going mad).

Especially, in the case of partner based DV:

-the victim tells mistruths to family and friends to avoid telling the truth about forced,
 manipulated, and prescribed, isolation produced from partner abuse/gaslighting

-hoovering (when the V of G attempts to leave the relationship, for instance, the gaslighter
 uses trigger words symbolising love, and endless promises, to stop the departure).

Signs of gaslighting from family members:

Firstly, the causes- gaslighting from parents, family members:

toxic parenting

abusive parenting

authoritarian (to the extreme) parenting

narcissistic parents or family members

Examples- gaslighting from parents, family members:

-"I won't tell you exactly what is said about you, but everyone in our family thinks it"

-" you are nothing"

-"you have never done anything right"

-"you are not one of us"

-"if you loved us, you would do what we say"

-"you are mad and we are only trying to help you"

-"none of your friends really like you, they are just pretending"

-"why would anyone want to befriend you?"

Signs of gaslighting from friends:

The causes- gaslighting from friends:

narcissism
jealousy
envy
practised splitting behaviors
revenge
hate
co-dependancy

Indicators- gaslighting from friends:

-(minimal to) nil displays of respect

-insincere verbalisations and actions

-constantly trying to control conversations, and the gaslighting victim

-spreads gossip (true secrets; and false/lies) to others in the friendship group (and beyond)

-manipulates

-attempts/achieves intimacy (as power play) with the victim's partner, or family members

-isolates the V of G from other friends

-is exhausting, emotionally demanding, and unreciprocal regarding support

-competes frequently and denigrates the victim's gains and achievements whilst
 highlighting (or lying about) their own

-nil reciprocity (takes and never gives)

-incapacity for empathy

-is explicitly inauthentic

-either adulates or hates, there is no in-between (including labelling friends as either
 wonderful or awful)

-fuels fights within the friendship group, between you and your partner, or family
 members (the P of G lays the groundwork to groom your partner, family members, and so
 forth, by befriending them and encouraging viewing them as their confidante).

Ultimately, what comes into question is Moral Injury:

".. a threat to core human needs ...involves transgressions against intrinsic moral imperatives. Moral injury is a particular type of psychological distress that can emerge following exposure to stressors known as potentially morally injurious events (PMIEs)".

(4)

Thus:

-(minimisation of) sense of purpose

-(causes self-questioning of) professional and personal integrity

-(contradictions to) ethics

-(compromisation of) one's own standards

-(exhaustion and damage beyond psychological realms)- to the core of self

-(questioning of) one's own moral stance (moral injury, and moral damage)

-moral disregard (of the victim, as with the points featured below)

-(unjustified) shame

-(induced and pernicious) regret

-(misplaced) guilt

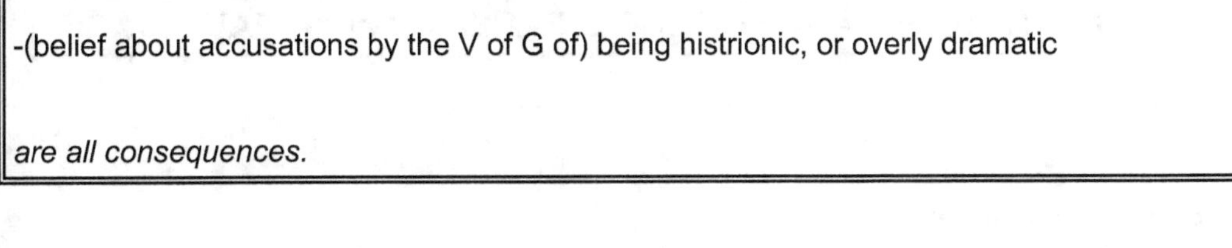

Vulnerability can lie in any form within life, where there is a power imbalance, which is misused and abused. So, too, with the focus in the next chapter.

Workplace gaslighting:

Institutional gaslighting:

"occurs within a company, organization, or institution, such as a hospital.
For example, they may portray whistleblowers who report problems as irrational or
incompetent, or deceive employees about their rights".
(5)

Workplace gaslighting includes the following elements:

-denying previous events

-refusing to admit that what they clearly stated to you, and even what was written in their
 work diary etc.

-persistent, unjustified negative comments about the V of G's performance

-gossip mongering directed specifically at you- the victim, and about you

-public denigration, and humiliation

-distorting, or minimising amount of information access, including availability
 or data regarding scheduled meetings

-the perpetration is usually fuelled by: insecurity, resentment and jealousy

-creating conflict between gaslightee and co-workers

-theft of ideas, work undertaken- passing it off as one's own

-creating a 'naming and shaming' work environment based upon lies and innuendo.

Thus, corporate/institutional/workplace gaslighting (with 'corporate/workplace stockholm syndrome' type symptoms) often incorporates:

-identification with the captor (manager, colleague) whilst in a hostage like situation (entrapped employee, co-worker) and doubting one's own (V of G's) sense of reality and perception of negative events, which are recurrent.

Patients- Medical gaslighting:

"Medical gaslighting takes many forms including someone telling another person they are imagining that they are ill or questions their sanity. Unfortunately, gaslighting is also performed by therapists and psychiatrists. Both can bring devastating results.
The problem of gaslighting is that it can have dire consequences leading to further harm or even the death of patients." (6 a)

This brings forth awareness of medical gaslighting and the dangerous impact of iatrogenesis (resultant medically induced harm), upon patients.

> "For once misunderstood, portrayed as something other than truthful, betrayed, put at risk, deceived, and their case covered-up, there comes a painful, ongoing journey of regret for ever trusting, confiding in, and seeking of (in any way) treatment..."
> (6 b)

Healthcare workers and effects of bullying/gaslighting:

> "Weaponisation:
>
> -use of the term 'burnout' colloquially to describe overwhelmed colleagues
>
> -to bully/bad mouth co-workers
>
> -for leaders to justify demotion, re-distribution of tasks, or return to work activities, which are demeaning or intended to block the worker from continuing in their job."
> (7)

Deficits in resources; defective healthcare systems; and, other human factors, often result in high levels of workplace stress.
When one is misdiagnosed with 'burnout' (7) by occupational departments, leaders, and colleagues, this can be perceived as a form of denial, and indeed gaslighting.

Gaslighting is a major factor in propagating recurrent and extensive moral injury (as discussed in previous pages), as the perpetrator (regardless of the fact that they are not relatives, part of chosen friendship groups, or intimate partners) seeks to convince you that it is 'all in your head'; that you are psychologically compromised; and, heading toward madness, whilst you are aware of the true reasons behind your distress and that you are being institutionally silenced.

The typical gaslighter displays the following characteristics:

25

-innate expectation of compliance from others, especially significant others

-need for admiration

-fear of abandonment

-hypersensitivity to criticism

-frequently labile mood; dependant upon level of compliance and submissiveness of V of G

-lack of true empathy

-prescribes goals in line with his/her's

-non-reciprocal in relationships, unless directly and personally advantageous

-lack of remorse

-need for power and control

-naturally manipulative persona

-given constantly to pathological lying

-P of G's continuity of motive and agenda (regarding the above variables).

There are 3 main types of gaslighters, according to Stern (2007).

The: glamour gaslighter; good guy gaslighter; intimidator gaslighter. (8)

An extrapolated, considered, description of each, follows.

'Glamour Gaslighter':

-initially (at the start of the relationship) they use charm, romance, and love-bombing. Ensuring similarity with likes, dislikes, opinions, interests of the target may also be involved.

-there may be evidence of insulting you in front of others, then a sudden turn toward compliments

-gift-giving post-gaslighting is common

-once ensconced in the relationship there is a sudden change to toxicity- gaslighting

-the perpetrator is very 'positive image of relationship' (as displayed to others) focussed.

'Good-guy Gaslighter':

-always (stating that he/she is) doing you a favour but accusations that you are ungrateful

-passive-aggressive in nature

-causes doubt and that you (as V of G) are delusional

-the gaslighting is often insecurity projection fuelled.

'Intimidator Gaslighter':

-classic gaslighting

-overtly belittles

-regularly bullies

-seeks to, and creates, guilty feelings

-withholds affection, discussion, and explanations.

GASLIGHTING INDICATORS

A clarification point is necessary: manipulative gaslighting versus
(the feminism inspired term) epistemic gaslighting (a sociological view, focussing on
elements of misogyny, for instance, which is presented as a cause of the gaslighting).

Epistemic gaslighting apparently involves, extreme play out of traditional gender roles; with women at a disadvantage and male power/toxic dominance over women; and, women considered lesser beings.
Nevertheless, this can be a justification used by men during manipulative gaslighting (either mental consciousness, or overtly vocalised, to the victim).

It is important to note, that what has been discussed in this publication, is primarily manipulative/mainstream gaslighting.

The focus here is that reasons for gaslighting do not (in the main) include learned behaviors (yes, they may have been modelled by one's own father, for instance, however, the choice is still made to impact a partner, colleague and so forth, later in life).

The following identifiers, of primary relevance, are summarised, accordingly:

-causes one to second guess their own reality, recall about previous events and conversations, and doubt their own stability, and feel that everything you do is wrong

-stockholm syndrome like responses in order to facilitate: cessation of gaslighting, attempt
to reason with the gaslighter; or, as an unconscious reaction to the gaslighting, frequently
occur.
It is a type of trauma bonding.

-labelling involves: that the victim is crazy, unstable, a liar, oversensitive, and misperceives
situations

-ongoing impacts and effects incorporate recruitment of friends, family members,
neighbors, work friends/colleagues, and communities .
The concept of contagion gaslighting; unwitting portrayal of extended gaslighting based
lies, opinions; and monikers/labels, is at issue here. It extends far beyond gossip, rumour,
and innuendo.

Naturally, with group-think contagion, one would have to possess core variables, and
propensity, to perpetrate the gaslighting to start with.

-shaming, creating isolation of the victim; projection and blame shifting; constant criticism/
disapproval

-often the gaslighter uses false counterbalancing techniques (like positive phrases,
or reinforcement) to continue luring the victim into interactions, compliance, or seeking
ongoing connection and feedback (a lure used to reinforce the victim's feelings and
thoughts that the gaslighter is not that bad, that they- the victim- must be imagining things,
is suffering from paranoia, or is indeed insane, or oversensitive).

Love-bombing is also a devised tactical strategy utilised by some P of Gs.

Thus, the gaslighting perpetrator:

-metaphorically strips you to the core, and beyond

-criticises habits, failings, idiosyncracies, etc.- whilst the perpetrator does not admit to
 their own failings

-makes you feel value-less: in relationships, friendships, with family members, to
 work colleagues, and in life

-criticises every move that you make, thoughts, opinions, actions, and decisions

-the P of G outright lies and refuses to admit to things inspite of clear evidence

-provides askewed reasons for their behavior as justification (and dismissal) for their
 comments and actions (this usually involves projecting of blame onto the victim)

-the gaslighter makes promises which are constantly broken.

GASLIGHTING EFFECTS

In addition to the 'stockholm syndrome' like symptoms aforementioned, there are many different gaslighting effects upon the gaslightee:

-poor self-esteem, and self-confidence; dubious about intuition; minimal to nil trust in self, judgement, and memory

-V of G's (via P of G and recruited others') belief that they are: mentally ill, inadequate, unstable, and useless.

Unsuccessful attempts at assertiveness, or setting of boundaries, with the gaslighter can: create guilty feelings in the victim; develop vulnerability and dependence; and typically, escalate the gaslighter to a more extreme level (for they perceive that they are losing control).

Long-term effects can include:

-trauma

-hopelessness

-continued dependence upon the P of G

-regularly defending the perpetrator's behaviors

-isolation.

Ultimately, the V of G moves quickly into 'survival mode'.

"The outcome of this survival mode or "freeze" reaction versus "fight" or "flight" reaction can result in a captive who experiences a loss of self-esteem, self-confidence, and psychological energy and who is "burned out" and too depressed to leave". (9 a)

Victim impact:

-feelings of insecurity

-upon the victim's attempts to be assertive or defend oneself the P of G reverses the situation and plays the victim

-puts self down in the relationship and in public domains

-apologises constantly

-seeks acceptance from the gaslighting perpetrator

-feelings of emotional and physical exhaustion

-(the victim is) lured back in (emotionally and psychologically) when receiving backhanded, to the benefit of the P of G (something undertaken to his/her benefit), or machiavellian, praise

-regular confusion

-guilty feelings due to the gaslighter projecting blame for misadventures onto you

-loss of friendships, family connection, and rejection by work colleagues, due to the perpetrator lying about you to others

-feeling isolated

-P of G publicly announces that you are mentally ill (with no true evidence of such)

-doubts about self-identity, including believing the perpetrator's claims that you are too
 emotional

-self-protection starts to involve telling mistruths to P of G to avoid the gaslighting
 behaviors

-irresolute regarding decision-making, own judgement, self-trust, and intuitive processes

-feelings of helplessness and hopelessness

-depression

-anxiety

-reliance upon others' to formulate own views, judgements and opinions

-embarrassment

-poor trust in others, and attachment issues, post-gaslighting relationship

-PTSD; CPTSD. (9 b)

STAGES of GASLIGHTING.

GHFSA: Grooming; Hostage to cruelty;
Fragmentation; revelationary Shock; Aftermath

The 5 newly created stages of manipulative/mainstream gaslighting: are (in some cases) sequentially interchangeable, especially stages 3 and 4.

A comprehensive explanation of each (victims') stage of **GHFSA: Grooming; Hostage to cruelty; Fragmentation; revelationary Shock; Aftermath** feature below:

Stage 1/ Grooming

-charm offensive

-usually, rapid progression of the relationship (feigned emotional intimacy, promotion of dependency, start of ingratiation with the gaslightee's significant others) with view to co-dependency

-highlighting the victim's idiosyncracies and faults (imagined or otherwise) as cute (etc.)

-dependant upon the type of gaslighter, gift-giving for personal gain or in the form of apology

-initiation of behavioral reinforcement (if the victim is 'good'- then reward; if the V of G
is considered 'bad/disobedient/too independent'- then consequences prevail)

-development of specific rules for the relationship (pertaining to desires and needs of
the gaslighter)

-initiation of minimising, questioning, or demeaning, choices made by the gaslightee
(this may be undertaken by the P of G in a subtle, jovial, or loving, way)

-the victim begins to excuse small signs of an unhealthy relationship to come (including
dismissal of one-sided perpetrator launched disagreements, as misunderstandings)

-the V of G is at the advent of acceptance that she/he is too sensitive.

Stage 2/ Hostage to cruelty

-heavy emotional and psychological (and physical intimidation, threats, or assault) tactics utilised by P of G

-stockholm syndrome like symptoms (please see 'Gaslighting Comprehensively Defined' chapter)

-resultant fear, apologies, and acquiescence (of the gaslightee)

-V of G's self-blame for P of G's toxic behaviors

-V of G's belief that they are stupid, guilty, disordered, and that this is the reason for trouble within the relationship, friendship, or work situation

-the gaslightee's seperation insecurity; fear of abandonment and rejection; and, relief-experienced, all at once

-feeling as if going insane (V of G)

-other mainstream symptoms, as previously mentioned.

Stage 3/ Fragmentation

-learned helplessness

-self-identity loss

-feeling more and more like 'a shell of a person'

-nil confidence in own judgement, decision making, or intuition

-disintegrating trust in self, others (aside from P of G)

-self-doubt

-indiscriminate isolation

-others comment that you have changed so much that you seem unrecognizable

-feeling as if have now become insane

-belief that you are a burden on the perpetrator, and to others

-concept that you deserve nothing better than the situation you are in

-inner strength, and other inner resources, have been dissipated to the point of
 mental and physical exhaustion

-moral injury.

Stage 4/ revelationary Shock

-hyperarousal, physical shaking (and with long-term abuse, experience of shaking
 internally)

-either speechless about the revelations/point of awareness, or locquaciousness

-panicked at the prospect of continued entrapment and abuse

-cognitive and relational bargaining, pleading, for the abuse to stop

-V of G vacillates between numbness and hypervigilance

-realisation of P of G's gaslighting tactics against you

-V of G's increased awareness that 'am not crazy' or imagining toxicity of the
 perpetrator

-feelings of betrayal

-increased comprehension that you are a victim of abuse/gaslighting (though may
 be conceptualised or termed differently)

-desire to escape the situation, but feel that there may be no easy way out

-awareness of moral injury (V of G).

Stage 5/ Aftermath

-continued feelings of betrayal enhanced by escalating anger and disgust (the victim)

-feelings of betrayal (by V of G) are long-term, potentiated when the gaslighter has
managed to elicit disloyalty from friends, family members, and previously trusted others

-avoidance of relationships, acquaintances, and social interactivity

-long-term trauma related symptomatology

-(consistent with the above point when serious physical harm, sexual assault, or death,
is threatened or in the former two actualised): PTSD or, CPTSD (9 b)

-depression and/or anxiety (though this can occur in earlier stages- the victim may be
plagued with these long-term issues)

-perception that everyone (including strangers) knows that you are/have been a victim

-V of G's fear that everyone will think that you are weak; mad; or, unworthy of: living a
fulfilling life; developing healthy friendships and relationships; and, having future
aspirations and dreams

-intrusive cognitions, such as you have been punished for just being you (and usually,
the best 'you' possible)

-not liking who you have/had become (V of G's vulnerability to dominance, abuse, and had slowly recognised that gaslighting was occuring)

-judgementalism (and suspicion) of others due to mistrust and anxiety that you will become a victim of gaslighting again (eg one thing wrongly done- or said- by another person may render them unforgivable and even dangerous, in your eyes)

-due to indoctrinated thought- leading to co-dependancy- the V of G prematurely (or immediately) indiscriminantly seeks another intimate relationship

-prolonged moral injury.

There are numerous, but quite standardised, gaslighting phrases which malignant narcissists, sociopaths and psychopaths (in particular) use to silence you.

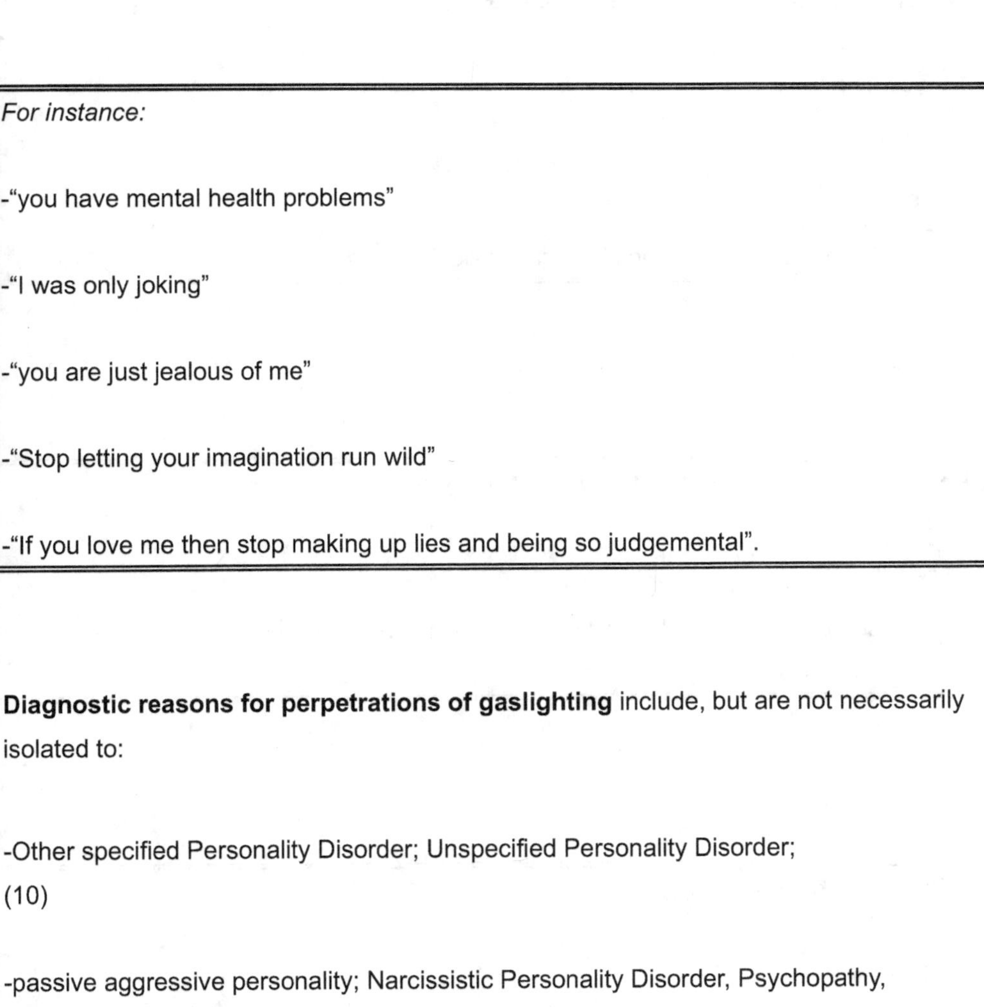

For instance:

-"you have mental health problems"

-"I was only joking"

-"you are just jealous of me"

-"Stop letting your imagination run wild"

-"If you love me then stop making up lies and being so judgemental".

Diagnostic reasons for perpetrations of gaslighting include, but are not necessarily isolated to:

-Other specified Personality Disorder; Unspecified Personality Disorder;
(10)

-passive aggressive personality; Narcissistic Personality Disorder, Psychopathy,
  Sociopathy and, authoritarianism

-inaccuracy in view of self, and interpersonal dysfunction, aspects (11) are also involved.

__The following assessment measures, are useful in identification of the existence of gaslighting:__

Are you being Gaslighted? (Gaslight Checklist)

-yes/no answers

-20 items

-self-report

-useful for both current and historical gaslighting experiences. (8)

SOPAS: Subtle and Overt Psychological Abuse Scale

-35 items

-measures psychological abuse undertaken in a loving, joking, or serious way (subtle or overt). (12)

the Abusive Behavior Inventory

-30 items

-measures both physical and psychological abuse

-initially created to assess a domestic violence based program. (13)

<u>**SSS: the Stockholm Syndrome Scale**</u>

-49 items

-measures core stockholm syndrome; psychological damage; love-dependence. (14)

<u>**MISS-HP: the Moral Injury Symptom Scale- Healthcare Professionals' version**</u>

-10 items

-measures elements such as: guilt, betrayal, moral concerns, shame, loss of meaning and purpose, self-condemnation, difficulty with forgiveness, changes to religious beliefs, loss of trust, and, loss of spiritual faith. (15)

CASE SCENARIO 1

1/ DV and family

-stockholm syndrome type symptoms present (in the V of G) for decades

-treated like an outsider by family, like she was not- genetically related- this element was most valued by family members to carry on the bloodline

-arranged marriage at 17 years of age- despite the cultural environment in which they resided (for more than 30 years) being contrary to this practise

-treated, perceived, and presented to others: like a pariah, intellectually compromised, a weak link, mad, and behaviorally abhorrent- for her entire life- by family members, and family friends, alike

-the V of G tried to reach out to extraneous family members for level of support

-inspite of family members' efforts she managed to legally gain (post-divorce from the abusive arranged marriage partner) enough finances to purchase an asset

-this insensed the family members no end, and they constantly chided, derided her for this, and pressured her (disregarding her youthful age and vigour) regarding testament and will based endeavours (naturally, advantageous to the immediate perpetrating family members involved)

-the constant, lifelong gaslighting based abuse had severe ramifications upon her physiological, emotional and psychological, well-being

-furthermore, for several decades the family members (on the basis of perverse loyalty, imagined indebtedness, and cultural entrapment) managed to inculcate themselves in every area of her life; including the victim dreading every interaction with them, but subjecting herself every 3rd day to the abuse that they constantly dealt her

-inter-generational familial recruitment of gaslighting against her also frequently occurred, including whereby her trusted younger relative became recruited for the 'greater gain and allegiance'

-nevertheless, her pursuit of truthfulness, honesty, integrity, and an enduring awareness (inspiring given that she had been exposed to gaslighting for so long) that her family were acting in extremely iniquitous ways, propelled her forward regardless

-she embarked upon her own successful studies, career, and profession

-though extremely traumatised, self-deprecating, and bearing the scars of gaslighting

-due to (it is argued) her endurance, commitment and recognition in others of integrity, honesty, and kindness, she managed to break the cycle of gaslighting abuse (in her late 40s) and partnered with a man, although protective (but positively so), who was the antithesis of all that her family, and kinship based connections, personified and perpetrated.

2/ Personal life (friendship)

Grooming, manipulation, and relentless pursuit of meeting own needs (perpetrator):

-texts: relentless texts focussing on own troubles, successes

-creation of self-doubt, deriding and complimenting intermittently, talking double dutch with expectations that the gaslightee will understand (and when they did not, that they were lesser, stupid, or not up to the standard of the gaslighter)

-competitive: unjustifiable professional prowess over victim

-claims of superiority of thought, life plan and actions

-opportunistically extroverted, narcissistic, and brazen

-further infused by displaced guilt due to past display of workplace weakness in the face of P of G induced conflict (in which both the gaslighter, gaslightee and others were involved)

-self-gain based social interaction.

Impact on gaslighter:

-professional connections lost

-loss of one part of livelihood; and, sacked from job (unique situation as many gaslighters manage to charm their way out of misadventure)

-financial/funding based personal gain: not by happenstance, funding oriented for both personal gain, and professional profit

-subterfuge, odious connections, new success: due to machiavellian planning, deceit, and nefariousnous, regarding existing networks- managed to reinvent self professionally (minus that partial loss of livelihood).

<u>Impact on gaslightee:</u>

-career sabotage: victim's loss of entire livelihood

-aftermath: involved additional people in the gaslighting endeavours whereby the victim remains emotionally and psychologically at the mercy of the subsequent gaslighters.

CASE SCENARIO 3

3/ Hostage (workplace)

-location of crime: club with gaming equipment

-multiple workers in the club were approached by a man with a high power rifle

-the manager approached the perpetrator in order to take responsibility for staff's safety

-both the manager, and 3 workers, were locked in a room, with the perpetrator (who was still threatening them with the high powered rifle)

-the room/ safe was small, appeared to lack much air filtration/air inlets

-the manager managed to negotiate with the perpetrator that his 3 staff were released without harm, following a stand-off of 4 hours

-the manager continued to be detained as a hostage for 13 hours, negotiating with police on the perpetrator's behalf

-during this time he was physically assaulted, threatened, and gaslighted, constantly

-the perpetrator decided to give himself up to police voluntarily (regardless of the police not having: entered the building nor threatened the perpetrator's survival)

-the manager, to this day, continues to suffer from recurrent nightmares, flashbacks, and all other relevant trauma related symptomatology, involving the abuse which he suffered

-though he is aware that the perpetrator had perpetrated a frightening, and illegal, act, the victim (manager) constantly tries to find reasons for the perpetrator's actions by way of quoting gaslighting terms which were used during the hostage taking.

CASE SCENARIO 4

4/ Whistleblowing blow back: school

-location: primary, elitist, religious secondary school

-so many sexual assaults and child sexual abuse (and suicides) were perpetrated that in the end they could not be obscured (a public inquiry ensued)

-gaslighting was so extreme that many students either left the school, or left 'in another way'

-one boy who had lost his father (to a questionably incurred death) at age 8 years, was sent to this school

-he had already suffered sexual abuse the year before (admission to the school), with his mother having seen yet, covered up the abuse

-he later disclosed that he too, was a victim of sexual abuse at the hands of the school; he identified, in no uncertain ways, his account of being gaslighted to the extreme throughout the process. His mother has yet to believe the claims, due to personal reasons, and the outright exclusivity of the school involved. This, unfortunately, is not unusual

-he witnessed many sexual assault based suicides of young, and very young, boys (from the rooftop)

-gaslighting was endemic, and perpetrated by: teachers, brothers, priests, lay staff, administration, and visiting staff (including medical professionals)

-many of the sufferers of the abuse, and subsequent (whistleblowing blow back) gaslighting, committed suicide, turned to drugs and alcohol abuse, or remained severely traumatised for their rest of their lives.

QUESTIONS regarding Causes, Symptoms, and Effects in the Gaslighting Case Scenarios

i) What are 3 key symptoms indicating gaslighting in each of the above scenarios?

ii) Name 3 unwritten/unspoken factors of importance for each case.

iii) Which of the victims of gaslighting (in the scenarios featured above) continue to display 'stockholm syndrome' like symptoms?

iv) In your opinion, who appears to have been the least evidently impacted by the gaslighting events?

v) Who seems to have been the most impacted by the gaslighting incidences?

vi) What are your recommendations for the victims in each of the scenarios?

KEY POINTS for COPING with GASLIGHTING

Naturally, there is no justification for gaslighting, it simply should not exist. Nor should anyone-ideally- be subjected to it, especially continuously.

However, when one is held prisoner/hostage to such insidious and poisonous behaviors, the following coping mechanisms and responses are often employed by sufferers:

* Seek support, especially if there is physical abuse or potential for, stalking, or other dangers- seek professional advice. One may not be able to foresee nor predict the reaction of the P of G.

To re-iterate, seek professional advice, before undertaking any of the following:

-discover and affirm self-worth, worthiness of being loved, and deserving of healthy, respectful relationships

-* break the silence and secrecy (discuss the situation with trusted others)

-trust one's own belief about incidences (or learn to trust)

-* make written notes about the gaslighting intricacies (and store them in a place where they cannot be accessed by the P of G)

-practise creating and maintaining clear boundaries with trusted others

-* seek information regarding gaslighting (via books, trusted resources) (again, store them away from the P of G)

-learn, and practise (with trusted others/not gaslighter) assertiveness skills

-self-reflection (self-awareness, not defined by the gaslighter)

-* time away (even if it is in the garden, for a short walk)

-learn to trust your intuition

-seek family, independent friendships', support

-* when secrecy is chosen, utilise discretionary and safe secrecy (from gaslighter) until one is able to remove self from the situation

-* leave the situation (to re-iterate: seeking support is a must, it is not recommended to undertake this on your own. If there is physical abuse or potential for, stalking, or other dangers- seek professional advice before undertaking this)

-hold onto the truth of self

-reframe (eg learning about toxic people is useful for the future)

-* connection with the outside world, even if you do not actively participate: via social media (independent of gaslighter's connections), viewing television news, and so forth assists in re-affirming reality

-visualise what it would be like out of the relationship

-* as one rebuilds the self, and successfully employs some of the abovementioned strategies, the desire for- and risk of- confrontation with the gaslighter increases. There are negatives and positives to confronting the gaslighter.

The negatives include:
the fact that the gaslighter will deny all of which they are accused; they will feel satiated in achieving upset to this level; anger and frustration will escalate in both perpetrator and victim; and the perpetrator may escalate to perilous levels.

However, some argue that the positives involve: the gaslighter will see that you reject his/her presented reality, their perverse rules, or conditional love/acceptance; that, you (the victim): have a bigger world that reflects the truth; have outside support; know that what you are experiencing is real; will not accept power, dominance and abuse; have the capacity to be assertive and self-trusting; and, that you are strong enough to leave the toxic relationship.

CPTSD: Complex Post Traumatic Stress Disorder

DV: Domestic Violence

etc.: etcetera

eg: (exempli gratia) for example

MISS-HP: the Moral Injury Symptom Scale- Healthcare Professionals' version

P of G: Perpetrator of Gaslighting

PTSD: Post-traumatic Stress Disorder

SOPAS: Subtle and Overt Psychological Abuse Scale

SSS: the Stockholm Syndrome Scale

V of G: Victim of Gaslighting

1/ In which year was Gaslighting announced as the 'word of the year'?

2/ Provide a general definition of 'gaslighting'.

3/ In thinking of gaslighting relating to workplace settings, name 3 ways in which the P of G achieves his/her aim.

4/ What is achieved by the gaslighter establishing herself/himself as an authority figure?

5/ Describe 2 ways in which the V of G relies upon the gaslighter's judgement.

6/ What propagates a cycle of gaslighting abuse?

7/ Please provide 5 stockholm syndrome like symptoms.

8/ Underlying reasons for V of G's stockholm syndrome like symptoms include:

    a) capture bonding

    b) depleted emotional resources

    c) cognitive-emotional bargaining

    d) all of the above.

9/ What is your understanding of 'neuroplasticity' and its relationship with trauma?

10/ What is considered a form of psychological terrorism?

11/ How does a gaslighter achieve his/her aim:
 	
    a) telling you to 'just let it go'
 	
    b) interrogation
 	
    c) silent treatment
 	
    d) all of the above.

12/ What results from the P of G's expectation that the V of G take responsibility for incidences?

13/ Provide an example of the gaslighter's minimisation and trivialization of the victim's concerns, belief, and persona.

14/ What is 'hoovering'?

15/ Describe the causes of gaslighting from family members.

16/ Give 3 examples of gaslighting by parents.

17/ Friends who gaslight typically undertake this, because of:

a) revenge

b) co-dependancy

c) comraderie

d) a) and b)

e) all of the above.

18/ What is your understanding of splitting behaviors in friendship groups?

19/ Have you directly experienced splitting behaviors amongst friends? If so, please provide a 10 word description of the impacts.

20/ How does gaslighting in friendship differ from that of parental based perpetrations?

21/ What is 'moral injury'?

22/ Provide 5 different effects of gaslighting based moral injury.

23/ How is power imbalance manipulated to create vulnerability?

24/ Describe 'institutional gaslighting'.

25/ Have you ever experienced, or witnessed, workplace gaslighting?

26/ In which way can minimising the amount of information access realise the P of G's aim, in the workplace setting?

27/ What typically fuels gaslighting in the work environment?

28/ Describe occupational 'naming and shaming'.

29/ Stockholm syndrome like symptoms can occur in the corporate

sector via:

a) employee entrapment

b) mistrusting one's sense of reality

c) identification with the captor

d) all of the above.

30/ Which of the factors (in the above question), if any, propagate

a continuation of stockholm syndrome like symptoms?

31/ Summarise the term 'medical gaslighting'.

32/ What is 'iatrogenesis'?

In which ways do you think it is relevant to medical gaslighting?

33/ How can 'burnout' be weaponised in the healthcare arena?

34/ Which factors may be present as the underlying reasons for misperceived burnout?

35/ Describe the concept of 'institutional silencing'.

36/ What is meant by 'profiling (of) gaslighters'?

37/ The typical gaslighter, is:

a) lacking in true empathy

b) very truthful

c) hypersensitive to criticism

d) a) and c)

e) all of the above.

38/ Think of a P of G, of which you are aware, and apply some of the standard gaslighting characteristics.

39/ (further to the above question) Inscribe a formulaic representation/ time line of the ways in which the gaslighter achieved her/his objectives.

40/ Which factors can determine the P of G's mood?

41/ There are 3 main types of gaslighters proposed. Please name them.

42/ (extrapolation of) Name the type of gaslighter who utilises the the following tactics:

i/ love-bombing ....

ii/ passive-aggression............................

iii/ overt belittling...................................

iv/ gift-giving......................................

v/ stated favours..............................

vi/ insults then compliments............................

vii/ withholds affection...................................

viii/ promotes positive image of relationship...........................

43/ Which of the 3 gaslighter types have you encountered?

44/ Explain how you dealt with the P of G (as abovementioned).

45/ What is meant by 'epistemic gaslighting'?

46/ Name another form (of focus) other than epistemic gaslighting.

47/ Do you believe that gaslighting involves learned behaviors.
Please give reasons for your answer.

48/ What is 'trauma bonding'?

49/ Labelling constitutes that the V of G is:

a) oversensitive

b) mad

c) a liar

d) all of the above.

50/ Explicate your comprehension of 'contagion gaslighting', including the who, how, and why.

51/ How may the P of G continue to lure the V of G?

52/ Usually the P of G does not admit to their own failings. What do they undertake simultaneously?

53/ Describe the extent to which the gaslighting perpetrator makes the victim feel value-less.

54/ What may occur when the victim attempts to set boundaries with the P of G?

55/ Name 3 long-term effects of gaslighting.

56/ Provide detail of victim-oriented 'survival mode'.

57/ (gaslighting) Victim impact include:

a) machiavellianism

b) guilt

c) rejection by work colleagues

d) b) and c)

e) all of the above.

58/ How would you react if you heard your trusted co-worker described as 'mentally ill', by your manager, in a public forum?

59/ (further to the above question) Provide a step-by-step plan which incorporates your response to the incident.

60/ What may ensue when a V of G experiences feelings of helplessness and hopelessness?

61/ Describe PTSD.

62/ Provide your understanding of CPTSD.

63/ What are the (created) 5 stages of manipulative/mainstream
gaslighting?

64/ At which stage of gaslighting is 'Grooming'?

65/ Gaslighter based grooming consists of:

   a) behavioral reinforcement

   b) satiating desires and needs of P of G

   c) targetting of significant others

   d) a) and c)

   e) a) and b)

   f) b) and c)

   g) all of the above.

66/ Provide 4 indicators of gaslighting Stage 2.

67/ Please name the (gaslighting) stage involving learned helplessness.

68/ Which stage involves indiscriminate isolation?

69/ At which stage(s) is/are moral injury most evident?

70/   i/ disintegrating trust

        ii/ identity loss

        iii/ feelings of confirmed insanity

        iv/ mental and physical exhaustion

    occur at which gaslighting Stage?

71/ Give a comprehensive description of (gaslighting) Stage 4.

72/ Betrayal from friends, family members, and previously trusted others may occur at which stage?

73/ When does it become apparent, to the V of G, that they feel unworthy of living a fulfilling life?

74/ Provide an example of a V of G's intrusive cognitions.

75/ What is meant by 'judgementalism' in the context of suffering gaslighting abuse?

76/ What can indoctrinated thought lead to?

77/ At which point does prolonged moral injury become apparent?

78/ Exemplify 2 standardised gaslighting phrases used to silence a V of G.

79/ Name the gaslighting related assessment which measures psychological abuse (perpetrated in a loving, joking, or serious way).

80/ Which gaslighting measure examines both physical and psychological abuse?

81/ Provide 3 elements involved in assessment process by way of the MISS-HP.

82/ Is there any justification for gaslighting? Discuss accordingly.

83/ In your opinion, what are some of the advantages to seeking professional support as a V of G?

84/ Coping with gaslighting, in some instances, may involve:

a) self-trust: belief about incidences

b) seeking information about gaslighting

c) self-reflection

d) all of the above.

85/ What is meant by holding onto the 'truth of self'?

86/ How may an isolated V of G attempt to connect with the outside world?

87/ Imagine that you are suffering from gaslighting.
Write or draw a representation of visualisation of freedom from the gaslighting.

88/ Discuss some of the negatives involved in confrontation with a
P of G.

89/ Provide a step-by-step safety plan for a V of G who is attempting to
seek independent support against the gaslighting.

90/ What is the SSS assessment scale?

REFERENCES

(1 a) Merriam-Webster. com Dictionary (2023), Gaslighting,
www.merriam-webster.com/dictionary/gaslighting

(1 b) Duignan, B. (Dec 11, 2022), Encyclopaedia Brittanica Gaslighting,
www.britannica.com/gaslighting

(2) American Psychological Association (APA) Dictionary of Psychology (2023), Gaslight,
www.dictionary.apa.org/gaslight

(3) Tophus, M.D. (2022), The A to Z of Workplace Bullying: For the Healthcare Professional and Beyond, Germany: Hilphma Publications, p.23.

(4) Hagerty, S.L. & Williams, L.M. Moral injury, traumatic stress, and threats to core human needs in health-care workers: the COVID-19 pandemic as a dehumanizing experience, Clinical Psychological Science, Nov. 2022, 10(6): 1060-1082.

(5) Medical News Today, What is gaslighting?, medically reviewed by Sarpalli, V. & Huizen, J. updated jul14, 2022, www.medicalnewstoday.com

(6 a) Davis, S. Medical and mental health gaslighting and iatrogenic injury, Jun 8, 2020, CPTSD Foundation, www.cptsdfoundation.org/2020/06/08/medical-and-mental-health-gaslighting-and-iatrogenic-injury/

(6 b) Tophus, M. D. (2023), The controversy of the remorseless and unempathic healthcare worker, Germany: Hilphma Publications, p.35.

(7) Tophus, M. D. (2022), Burnout in healthcare, Germany: Hilphma Publications, p.38.

(8) Stern, R. (2007), The Gaslight Effect: how to spot and survive the hostile manipulation others use to control your life, New York, NY: Morgan Road books, pp. 5-6.

(9 a) Logan, M.H., Stockholm Syndrome: held hostage by the one you love, Violence and Gender, Feb 2018, 5(2), 67-69

(9 b) Tophus, M. D. (2022), Trauma united, life defined. A healthcare tool for professionals across the globe, Germany: Hilphma Publications.

(10) American Psychiatric Association (2022), Diagnostic and Statistical Manual of Mental Disorders, 5th ed. Text Revision: DSM-5-TR. Washington, D.C.: American Psychiatric Association Publishing.

(11) World Health Organization (2019), International Statistical Classification of Diseases and Related Health Problems, 11th ed,; ICD-11.

(12) Marshall, L.L. (2000), SOPAS: Subtle and Overt Psychological Abuse of women Scale, Available from Linda L. Marshall at the University of North Texas, Dept Psychology, 1155 Union Circle # 311280, Denton, Texas 76205-5017.

(13) Shephard, M.F. The Abusive Behavior Inventory: a measure of psychological and physical abuse, Journal of Interpersonal Violence, 1992, 7(3): 291-305.

(14) Graham, D.L., Rawlings, E.I., Ihms, K., Latimer, D., Foliano, J., Thompson, A., Suttman, K., Farrington, M. & Hacker, R. A scale for identifying "Stockholm syndrome" reactions in young dating women: factor, structure, reliability, and validity. Violence Vict. 1995 Spring; 10(1): 3-22.

(15) Mantri, S., Koenig, H.G., Wang, Z.Z. & Lawson, J. Identifying moral injury in healthcare professionals: the Moral Injury Symptoms Scale- HP. J Relig Health, 2020. 59, 2323- 2340.

INDEX

1938 11
1940 11
1944 11
abandonment 25; 36
abuse/d 12; 13; 39; 42; 44; 53; 54; 55
abuser 13
abusive behavior inventory 44
abusive parenting 17
accept 55
acceptance 32; 35; 55
access/ed 22; 53
accuracy 43
accusations 15; 16; 21; 26
accused 55
accusing 16
achievements 19
achieves 19
achieving 55
acquaintances 41
acquiescence 36
actions 11; 15; 18; 30
actively 55
activities 24
actualised 41
admiration 25
admit 22; 30
adulates 19
advantageous 25
advent 35
advice 53; 54
affection 27
affirm 53
aftermath 34
agenda 25
all in your head 24
alliance 13
ambivalence 13
anger 41; 55
announces 33
anxiety 33; 41; 42
anyone 18
anything 17
apologies 36
apologises 32
apologize 16
apology 34

appeasement 14
approval 12
argument 16
aspects 43
aspirations 41
assault 36
assertive/ness 31; 32; 54; 55
assessment 44
assists 55
attachment/s 14; 33
authoritarian/ism 17; 43
authority 12; 14
availability 22
avoid 17; 33
avoidance 41
aware/ness 23; 24; 39
away 54
backhanded 32
bad 29; 35
bad mouth 24
bargaining 14; 39
basic needs 13
befriend/ing 18; 19
behavior 30
behavioral reinforcement 35
behaviors 14; 18; 28; 31; 36; 42; 53
belief/s 12; 36; 37; 45; 53
believed 16
believing 33
belittles 27
belittling 11
benefit 32
betrayal 39; 41; 45
betrayed 24
better 38
blame 16; 30; 32
blame shifting 29
block 24
blow back 51
bonding 13
books 54
boundaries 31; 53
brainwashing 14
break 53
broken 30
bullies 27
bully 24
burden 37
burned out 32

burnout 24
capacity 12
captive 13; 32
captor 13; 23
capture 13
case 24
cause 28
cessation 29
change/s/d 37; 45
characteristics 25
charm 26; 34
choice/s 28; 35
chosen 54
claims 33
clarification 28
classic 27
clear 30; 53
co-dependancy 18; 34; 42
cognitions 41
cognitive 14; 39
cognitive-emotional 14
colleague/s 23; 24; 28; 29
colloquially 24
comment/s 22; 30; 37
commitment 11
common 26
communities 29
company 22
competes 19
compliance 25; 29
compliments 26
comprehension 39
comprehensive 34
compromisation 20
compromised 24
concept/ualised 14; 38; 39
conceptually 14
concerns 45
conditional 55
confabulated 15
confidante 19
confidence 11; 37
confiding 24
conflict 23
confrontation 55
confusion 11; 15; 32
connection/s 12; 29; 32; 55
consequences 21; 23; 35
consistent 41

constantly 16; 18; 30; 32
contact 12
contagion gaslighting 29
continuing 24
continuously 53
contradictions 20
control 18; 25; 31
conversational 28
conversations 11; 18
convince 24
coping 53
core 20; 29; 30
corporate 23
counterbalancing 29
covered up 24
co-workers 23
CPTSD 33; 41; 56
crazy 29; 39
creates 27
creating 53
criticises 30
criticism 25; 29
current 44
cute 34
cycle 12
damage 20; 45
dangerous 23; 42
dangers 53; 54
data 22
death 23; 41
deceive/d 22; 24
decision making 15; 33; 37
decisions 11; 30
de-escalating 14
defective 24
defend/ing 31; 32
deficit/s 16; 24
deleterious 15
delusional 26
demanding 19
demeaning 24; 35
demotion 24
denial 16; 24
denigrates 19
denigration 22
deny/ing 22; 55
departure 17
dependence 31; 34
dependency 34

depressed 32
depression 33; 41
deserve 38
deserving 53
desire/s 35; 40; 55
desparation 14
deteriorating 12
devastating 23
development 35
difficulty 45
dire 23
direct/ly 12; 25
disadvantage 28
disagreements 35
disapproval 29
discover 53
discretionary 54
discuss/ion 27; 53
disgust 41
disintegrating 37
dislikes 26
dismissal 35
disobedient 35
disordered 36
displayed 26
disregard 20
dissipate/s/d 12; 38
distorting 22
distress 20; 24
domains 32
domestic violence 44
dominance 28; 42; 55
domination 12
doubt/s 11; 15; 26; 28; 33
doubting 23
dramatic 21
dreams 41
dubious 31
DV 17; 46; 56
dysfunction 43
elements 22; 45
embarrassment 33
emerge 20
emotional 32; 34; 36
emotional resources 14
emotional/ly 11; 13; 19; 32
empathy 19; 25
employee/s 22; 23
encouraging 19

endless 17
energy 32
enhanced 41
ensconced 26
entrapment 39
entrapped 23
envy 18
epistemic gaslighting 28
errors 11
escalate/s 31; 55
escalating 41
escape 40
ethics 20
events 11; 22; 23; 28
everyone 17; 41
everything 28
evidence 26; 30; 33
excuse 35
exhausting 19
exhaustion 20; 32; 38
exist 53
existence 44
expectation 25
expecting 16
experience 39
experiences 11; 32; 44
experiencing 55
explanations 27
explicitly 19
exposure 20
extended 29
extensive 24
extrapolated 26
extreme 28; 31
facilitate 29
factors 14
failings 30
faith 45
false 19; 29
false memories 15
family 17; 32; 46; 54
family members 17; 19; 29; 30; 41
father 28
faults 34
favour 26
fear 15; 25; 36; 41
feedback 11; 29
feel/ing/s 27; 28; 29; 30; 31; 32; 33; 37; 39; 40; 41; 55
feigned 34

feminism 28
fight/s 19; 32
flight 32
focus/sed 21; 26
forced 17
foresee 53
forgetfulness 15
forgiveness 45
formulate 33
fragmentation 34; 37
freeze 32
friends 17; 18; 19; 29; 30; 32
friends 41
friendship/s 36; 48; 41; 54
friendship group/s 19; 24
frustration 55
fuel/ling/led 19; 23; 26
fulfilling 41
further 23
future 41; 54
gain/s 19; 34
garden 54
gaslight checklist 44
gender 16; 28
GHFSA 34
gift-giving 26; 34
gives 19
glamour gaslighter 26
goals 25; 35
good boy 14
good girl 14
good guy gaslighter 26
gossip 19; 29
gossip mongering 22
groom 19
groom/ing 19; 34
groundwork 19
group-think 29
guilt 45
guilt/y 20; 27; 31; 32; 45
habits 30
happened 15
harm 23; 41
hate/s 18; 19
healthcare systems 24
healthy 41; 53
help 16; 18
helplessness 33
highlighting 19; 34

historical 44
histrionic 21
hoovering 17
hopelessness 31; 33
horrible 19
hospital 22
hostage 23; 50; 53
hostage to cruelty 34; 36
human 20
human factors 24
humanisation 13
humiliation 22
hyperarousal 39
hypersensitivity 25
hypervigilance 39
iatrogenesis 23
ideas 23
identification 23; 44
identifiers 28
identifying 13
identity 37
idiosyncracies 30; 34
ill 23
image 26
imagination 43
imagined 34
imagining 16; 23; 29; 39
imbalance 21
immediately 42
impact/s 15; 23; 28; 29; 32
inadequate 31
inauthentic 19
incapacity 19
incompetent 22
independent 35; 54; 55
indirect 12; 20
indiscriminantly 42
indiscriminate 37
indoctrinated 42
ineffective 15
information 22; 54
ingratiation 34
initially 26
initiation 35
innate 25
inner 38
innuendo 11; 23; 29
insane 29; 36; 37
insecurity 23; 26; 32; 36

insidious 53
insincere 18
institution/al/ally 11; 22; 24
insulting 26
intended 24
interactions 29
interactivity 41
interchangeable 34
interests 26
intermittent 14
interpersonal 43
interrogation 15
intimacy 19; 34
intimate 16; 24; 42
intimidation 36
intimidator gaslighter 26; 27
intricacies 53
intrinsic 20
intrusive 41
intuition 31; 37; 54
intuitive 33
irrational 22
irresolute 33
isolate/s/d 17; 19; 33; 43
isolation 29; 31; 37
issues 33; 41
items 16; 44; 45
jealous/y 18; 23; 43
job 24
joking 15; 43; 44
journey 24
jovial 35
judgement 12; 31; 33; 37
judgemental/ism 42; 43
justification 28; 30; 53
justify 11; 24
kindness 16
labelling 19; 29
labels 29
labile mood 25
lack 25
leaders 24
learn/ed 28; 53; 54
learned helplessness 37
learning 54
leave 32; 54; 55
lesser 28
let it go 15
level/s 31; 55

liar 29
lies 17; 19; 23; 29; 30; 43
life 21; 28; 30; 41; 48
likes 26
living 41
locquaciousness 39
longevity 13
long-term 31; 39; 41
losing 31
loss 16; 32; 37; 45
love/d 16; 17; 53; 55
love-bombing 26; 29
love-dependence 45
loving 35; 44
lured 32
luring 29
lying 11; 15; 16; 19; 25; 29; 32
machiavellian 32
mad/ness 16; 18; 24; 41
mainstream 28; 36
maintaining 53
male 28
malignant 43
managed 41
manager 23
manipulate/ion 11; 12
manipulate/s/d 17; 19
manipulative 25; 34
manipulative gaslighting 28; 34
meaning 45
measures 44
mechanisms 53
medical gaslighting 23
medically induced 23
meetings 22
memories 11
memory 12; 16; 31
mental 11; 38
mental health 43
mental illness 11
mental state 12
mentally 28
mentally ill 31; 33
metaphorically 30
mimicking 16
minimal 18
minimising 16; 22; 35
misadventures 32
misdiagnosed 24

misogyny 28
misperceives 29
misplaced 16; 20
MISS-HP 45; 56
mistrust 42
mistruths 33
misunderstandings 35
misunderstood 24
misused 21
mocking 15
mode 32
modelled 28
monikers 29
moral 20; 45
moral injury 20; 24; 38; 40; 42
motive 25
move on 15
naming and shaming 23
narcissism 18
narcissist/s/ic 17; 43
narcissistic personality disorder 43
need/s 20; 25; 35
negative/s 11; 22; 23; 55
neighbors 29
neuroplasticity 14
news 55
non-reciprocal 25
norm/alised 12; 14
notes 53
nothing 15; 17
numbness 39
numerous 43
occupational departments 24
occur 41
offensive 34
ongoing 24; 29
opinions 26; 29; 30; 33
organizational 22
outcome 32
outside 55
over-sensitive 16; 29
overt/ly 27; 28; 44
overwhelmed 24
painful 24
panicked 39
paranoia 29
participate 55
participation 13
partner/s 17; 19; 24; 28

passive-aggressive 26
pathological 25
patients 23
people 54
perceive/d 24; 31
perception/s 11; 23; 41
performance 22
perilous 55
pernicious 20
persistent 22
persona 25
personal 12; 34; 48
personal- integrity 20
personality disorder 43
personally 25
perverse 55
phrases 29; 43
physical 14; 32; 36; 38; 39; 41; 44; 53; 54
plagued 41
playing 15
pleading 39
PMIEs 20
point 39
poisonous 53
portray/s/ed 22; 24
portrayal 29
positive/s 26; 29; 55
post-gaslighting 26; 33
potential 53
potentiated 41
power 21; 25; 28; 55
power play 19
practise 53
predict 53
prematurely 42
preparedness 14
prescribed 17; 25
pretending 18
primary 28
prisoner 53
problem/s 16; 22; 23; 43
processes 33
professional 53; 54
professional- integrity 20
program 44
progression 34
projected 16
projecting 30; 32
projection 26; 29

prolonged 42
promises 17; 30
promotion/al 34
propagating 24
propensity 29
prospect 39
proximity 14
psychiatric 11
psychiatrists 23
psychological/ly 11; 13; 14; 15; 20; 24; 32; 36; 44; 45
psychopaths 43
psychopathy 43
PTSD 33; 41; 56
public/ly 11; 22; 32; 33
punished 41
punishment 11
purpose 20; 45
questioning 35
questions 23
race 16
rapid 34
reaction 14; 29; 32; 53
re-affirming 55
real 55
realisation 39
reality 11; 23; 28; 55
realms 20
reason/s 24; 29; 30; 43; 36
rebuilds 55
recall 28
reciprocity 19
recognise 42
recommended 54
recruited 31
recurrent 23; 24
re-distribution 24
reflects 55
reframe 54
refuses 30
refusing 22
regret 20; 24
regularly 27
reinforcement 29
reject/ion 32; 36; 55
relational 39
relationship/s 12; 16; 17; 25; 26; 30; 32; 33; 34; 35; 36; 55; 41; 42; 53
relatives 24
release 14
relevance 28

reliance 12; 13; 33
relief 14; 36
religious 45
remorse 25
remove 54
report 22
resentment 23
resources 24; 38; 54
respect 18
respectful 53
response/s 13; 29; 53
responsibility 16
result/s 23; 24; 32
resultant 36
return to work 24
revelationary shock 34; 39
revelations 39
revenge 18
reverses 32
reward 14; 35
right 17
rights 22
risk 24; 55
roles 28
romance 26
rules 35; 55
rumour/s 11; 29
sabotage 11
safe 54
sanity 11; 23
satiated 55
scaring 15
scheduled 22
schema 14
school 51
screaming 15
second guess 28
secrecy 53; 54
secrets 19
seek/ing 16; 24; 29; 53; 54
seeks 27; 32
self 20; 31; 37; 43; 54; 55
self-awareness 54
self-blame 36
self-condemnation 45
self-confidence 31; 32
self-doubt 37
self-esteem 11; 12; 31; 32
self-identity 14; 33

self-protection 33
self-questioning 20
self-reflection 54
self-report 44
self-trust/ing 15; 33; 55
self-worth 53
sense 23
sensitive 35
seperation 36
serious 41; 44
setting 31
sexual assault 41
shaking 39
shame 20; 45
shaming 29
shell of a person 37
significant 15
significant others 25; 34; 44
signs 35
silence/d 24; 43; 53
silent treatment 15
similarity 26
simulated 14
situation/s 14; 29; 32; 36; 38; 40; 53; 54
skills 54
social 41
social media 55
sociological 28
sociopath/s/y 43
SOPAS 44; 56
specific 35
speechless 39
spiritual 45
splitting 18
spreads 19
SSS 45; 56
stability 11; 28
stage 34
stalking 53; 54
stance 20
standardised 43
standards 20
stated 22
stating 16
stockholm syndrome 12; 23; 29; 31; 36; 45
stop 17; 39; 43; 53
story 16
strangers 41
strategies 55

strategy 29
strength 38
stress 13; 24
stressors 20
strips 30
strong 55
stupid 16; 36
subjected 53
submissiveness 25
subtle 16; 35; 44
subversive 16
successfully 55
sudden 26
sufferers 53
suffering 29
support 19; 53; 54; 55
survival 13; 32
suspicion 42
symbolising 17
sympathizing 13
symptomatology 41
symptoms 12; 23; 31; 36
tactical 29
tactics 13; 36; 39
takes 19
target 11; 26
tasks 24
techniques 29
television 55
telling 15; 33
terrorism 15
theft 23
therapists 23
thought/s 11; 29; 30; 42
threat/s 12; 16; 20; 36
threatened 41
threatening 15
time 11; 13
time 54
toxic 28; 36; 42; 54; 55
toxic parenting 17
toxicity 26; 39
traditional 28
transgressions 20
trauma bonding 29
trauma/tic 14; 31; 41
treatment 24
trigger 17
trivialising 16

trouble 36
trust 12; 31; 33; 37; 45; 53; 54
trusted 41; 53
trusting 24
truth/ful 17; 24; 54; 55
turn 26
unconscious 13; 29
underlying 13
understanding 11
unforgivable 42
ungrateful 26
unhealthy 35
unjustified 20; 22
unreciprocal 19
unrecognizable 37
unstable 29; 31
unwitting 29
unworthy 41
upset 55
useful 54
useless 31
vacillates 39
validity 11
value-less 30
variables 25; 29
verbalisations 18
view/s 33; 43
visualise 55
vocalised 28
vulnerability 14; 21; 31; 42
walk 54
weak 41
weaponisation 24
whistleblowers 22
whistleblowing 51
withholds 27
women 28
wonderful 19
words 17
work 12; 36
work colleagues 30; 32
work diary 22
work environment 23
work friends 29
work performance 11
worker 24
workplace 22; 24; 50
world 12; 14; 55
worthiness 53

written 53
wrong 28; 42
wrote 22